SandCastle

Rhyme Time

A Calico
in the Window

Tracy Kompelien

Consulting Editor, Diane Craig, M.A./Reading Specialist

ABDO
Publishing Company

Published by ABDO Publishing Company, 4940 Viking Drive, Edina, Minnesota 55435.

Printed in the United States.

Credits
Edited by: Pam Price
Curriculum Coordinator: Nancy Tuminelly
Cover and Interior Design and Production: Mighty Media
Photo and Illustration Credits: BananaStock Ltd., Brand X Pictures, Digital Vision, Goodshoot.com, Hemera, Image 100, Tracy Kompelien, PhotoDisc, Stockbyte

Library of Congress Cataloging-in-Publication Data

Kompelien, Tracy, 1975-
    A calico in the window / Tracy Kompelien.
        p. cm. -- (Rhyme time)
    Includes index.
    ISBN 1-59197-778-9 (hardcover)
    ISBN 1-59197-884-X (paperback)
    1. English language--Rhyme--Juvenile literature. I. Title. II. Rhyme time (ABDO Publishing Company)

PE1517.K66 2004
428.1'3--dc22
                                                                    2004050797

SandCastle™ books are created by a professional team of educators, reading specialists, and content developers around five essential components that include phonemic awareness, phonics, vocabulary, text comprehension, and fluency. All books are written, reviewed, and leveled for guided reading, early intervention reading, and Accelerated Reader® programs and designed for use in shared, guided, and independent reading and writing activities to support a balanced approach to literacy instruction.

Let Us Know

After reading the book, SandCastle would like you to tell us your stories about reading. What is your favorite page? Was there something hard that you needed help with? Share the ups and downs of learning to read. We want to hear from you! To get posted on the ABDO Publishing Company Web site, send us e-mail at:

sandcastle@abdopub.com

SandCastle Level: Transitional

Words that rhyme do not have to be spelled the same. These words rhyme with each other:

calico   mow

doe   owe

domino   radio

grow

snow

know   window

Tessa waters a plant so that it will **grow**.

4

A cat with tan and black spots is called a **calico**.

Brad is looking out the window.

A female deer is called a doe.

Bart and Rachel like to play in the pool.

They both **know** how to swim.

Dane is holding a domino.

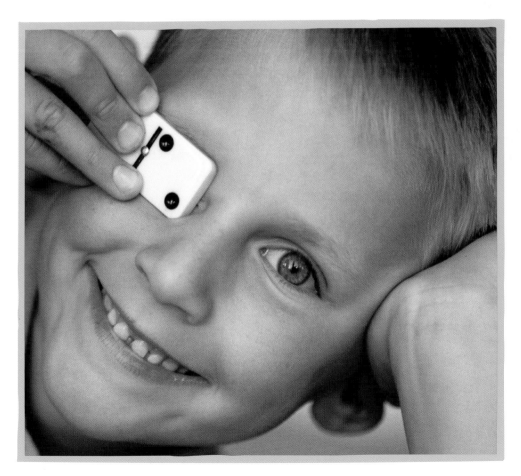

Robin pretends to mow the lawn with his toy lawn mower.

When Stella's family is finished grocery shopping, the cashier tells them how much they owe.

Allen and Connie are skiing with their mother on the snow.

Lance uses headphones to listen to his radio.

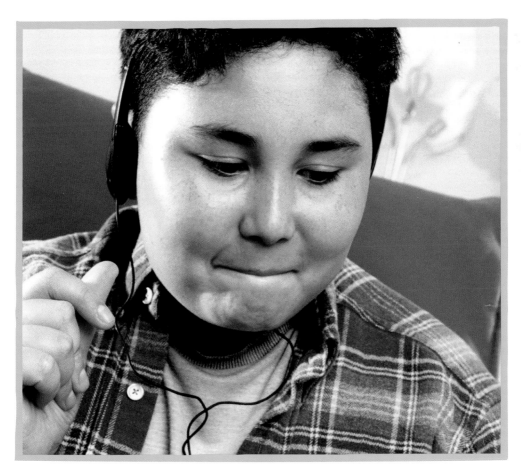

A Calico in the Window

Connie the calico
sure does know
how to catch a show
when sitting in the window.

Although today was slow,
she has seen quite a show.

While looking out the window,
the calico saw the neighbor mow.

Then she saw him begin to sow
pumpkin seeds he hoped would grow.

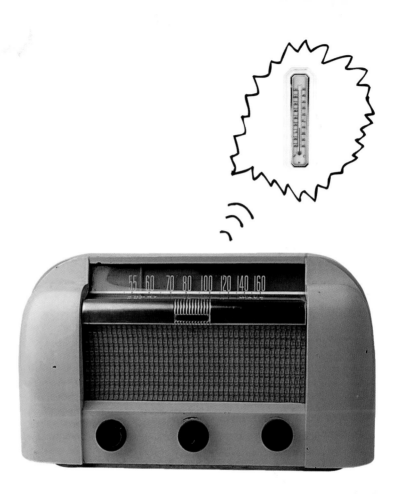

Inside, the news played on the radio.
The weather report said the temperature would be low.

Later in the day, the snow began to blow.

After the snow,
the window show became slow,
so Connie called Domino.

Connie the calico did glow
when she saw that Domino
was coming over to say hello.

Rhyming Riddle

What do you call a female deer in a blizzard?

Snow doe

Glossary

blizzard. a heavy snowstorm with very strong winds

cashier. the person who collects the money for things you buy at a store

domino. a flat, rectangular tile that is divided in half, with zero to six dots on each half

mow. to cut down grass, hay, or grain

sow. to scatter seeds over the ground so they will grow

temperature. the measurement of how hot or cold something is

About SandCastle™

A professional team of educators, reading specialists, and content developers created the SandCastle™ series to support young readers as they develop reading skills and strategies and increase their general knowledge. The SandCastle™ series has four levels that correspond to early literacy development in young children. The levels are provided to help teachers and parents select the appropriate books for young readers.

Emerging Readers
(no flags)

Beginning Readers
(1 flag)

Transitional Readers
(2 flags)

Fluent Readers
(3 flags)

These levels are meant only as a guide. All levels are subject to change.

To see a complete list of SandCastle™ books and other nonfiction titles from ABDO Publishing Company, visit www.abdopub.com or contact us at:
4940 Viking Drive, Edina, Minnesota 55435 • 1-800-800-1312 • fax: 1-952-831-1632